CREATE A VISION BOARD TO MANIFEST YOUR DREAMS

Instructions:

- Envision the life you want for yourself.

- Cut out elements (images, words, and affirmations) from the magazine that match your vision.

- Glue or tape the selected elements to a poster-board or a sheet of paper. You have now created a vision board!

- Look at your vision board and imagine what it would feel like to have everything you want come true. Stay in the energy as if you already have it, and the universe will align to make it so.

If you enjoy this magazine, please consider leaving me a positive review on Amazon to support me as an independent publisher. Thank you!

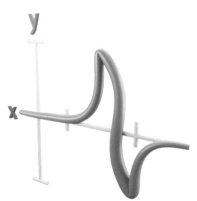

ONLINE SCHOOL

Great SAT Score

STUDY FOR SAT EXAM

GET GOOD GRADES

Study for ACT Exam

GREAT ACT SCORE

MAKE THE DEAN'S LIST

Go to Trade School

Go to College

HONOR ROLL

Make the Team!

SOCCER

Volleyball

Hockey

BASEBALL

Cross Country

BASKETBALL

Softball

Volleyball

WRESTLING

Cheer Squad

Swim

TENNIS

Football

Track & Field

RUGBY

JOIN THE CLUB!

Debate

ROTC

Chess

ROBOTICS

MATH

STUDENT GOVERNMENT

STEM

Green Club

HONOR'S SOCIETY

Band

SCIENCE

Study Group

Drama

SCHOOL NEWSPAPER

happy
GRADUATION

SUCCESS
→ go get it →

Success

Achievement

to be best
point of view
Achieve [ə't'
to perform
great enter

I HAVE RIZZ

Make New Friends

I am Popular

BUILD STRONG FRIENDSHIPS

NERDY AND I LOVE IT

Everyone Likes Me

No Cap

SQUAD GOALS

FIND MY STYLE

Bussin

BELIEVE IN MYSELF

B E S T
F R I E N D S
♥ ♥ ♥

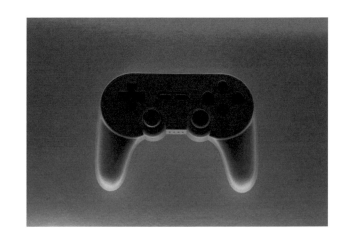

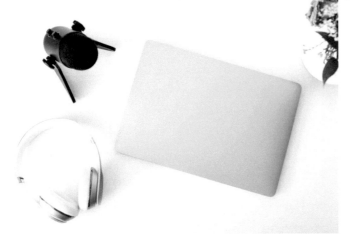

I Take Care
of Myself

START
GOOD
HABITS

I HAVE
CONFIDENCE
IN MYSELF

I Get
Enough
Rest

I AM
ACTIVE

I MAKE
GOOD CHOICES

My Future
is Bright

I AM
HEALTHY

I AM
HELPFUL

I am
Kind

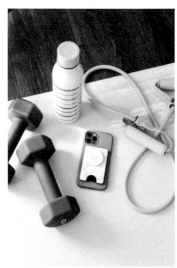

I Am Fit

I EAT
HEAL THY FOOD

I Exercise

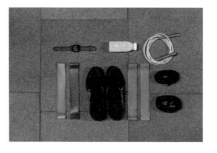

I am Manifesting:

NEW CLOTHES

A Bedroom Makeover

NEW SHOES

New Make-up

Laptop

GAMING COMPUTER

Tablet

MY OWN BEDROOM

Game System

Sunglasses

NEW PHONE

VR Headset

DRIVER'S LICENSE

A Car

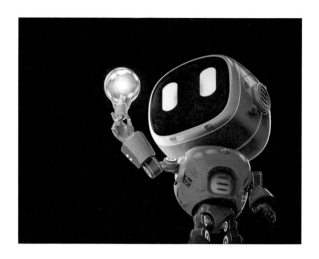

Self Care

SELF ♡ CARE

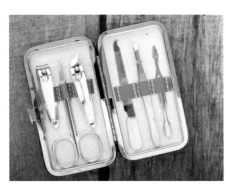

My eternal love,
I really had to write this letter
because I can't stop thinking abou
even if I try my hardest not to –
much as I know there isn't much
of distance betw
leave m

LOVE LETTER

LOVE

First Kiss

MY CRUSH
TEXTED ME

MY CRUSH
ASKED ME OUT

Babe

They Have a
Crush On Me

QUEEN

GIRLFRIEND

Love

Boyfriend

They Like
Me Too

I HAVE A DATE
TO THE DANCE

King

First
Love

We Are Going
On A Date

I AM LOVABLE

Find the
Perfect
Dress

Homecoming
Dance

Get My
Makeup Done

PROM KING

SPRING BREAK!

Summer break

R.E.L.A.X

The Perfect Summer

SUMMER JOB

DANCE

Ballet

Hip-Hop

13th
Birthday

**14th
Birthday**

BAR
MITZVAH

BAT
MITZVAH

Quinceanera

**15th
Birthday**

16TH
BIRTHDAY

SWEET 16

17th
Birthday

18TH
BIRTHDAY

19th Birthday

And so it will be.

Made in the USA
Columbia, SC
16 December 2024

49869259R00040